STRESS

STRESS

Biblical TRUTHS

— that —

Bring Peace

B&H
PUBLISHING GROUP

NASHVILLE, TENNESSEE

CONTENTS

CONTENTS

Somewhere along the line, the Bible attracted a reputation for being both irrelevant and impossible to understand. Out of touch as well as out of reach. Yet while conclusions like these continue to persist, so does human need for the Bible to be everything God affirms it to be: "living and effective" (Hebrews 4:12), its message "very near you, in your mouth and in your heart" (Deuteronomy 30:14).

If families and friends are to live together in unity . . . if lives are to be whole and fruitful in heart and mind . . . if tragedy and loss and disappointment and confusion are to be survived . . . no, not merely survived but transformed into peace and power and a purposeful way forward . . . you need a Word that is here and now and able to be grasped. You need to "know the truth," because "the truth will set you free" (John 8:32).

That's why you picked up this book. As the stress in your life becomes overwhelming, you need to take a step back and soak in God's Word.

Filled with Scriptures that speak personally to you this little book is further proof that God intends His Word to share living space with your present reality. Always in touch. Always within reach. No matter where you are, or what you are going through, allow this book to help direct you to the Scriptures you need most.

Sometimes it can feel like the entire world is against us. Everything is going wrong, and we are trapped in our circumstances. We become overwhelmed by the stress of the circumstances, or the idea of the future. But stress is not the end. God is for us; and if that is true who can be against us? Our eternal reassurance in the face of conflict, rejection, worry, and stress is that God's love for us is constant. No matter what kind of stress you find yourself in, let these verses reassure you of the one who is always on your side.

*But the L*ORD *said to Samuel, "Do not look at his appearance or his stature because I have rejected him. Humans do not see what the L*ORD *sees, for humans see what is visible, but the L*ORD *sees the heart."*

    1 Samuel 16:7

———

Everyone the Father gives me will come to me, and the one who comes to me I will never cast out.

    John 6:37

———

But God proves his own love for us in that while we were still sinners, Christ died for us.

    Romans 5:8

If God is for us, who is against us?
  Romans 8:31

———

Peter began to speak: "Now I truly understand that God doesn't show favoritism, but in every nation the person who fears him and does what is right is acceptable to him."
  Acts 10:34–35

Father, I am overwhelmed with stress. I am at the point where I feel trapped in doubt and despair. Thank You for Your constant presence through the valley, and for Your acceptance of me into Your family. Turn on the light so that I can find my way out of this place of despair. Continue to hold me in Your arms and never let me go. Amen

Anger at yourself, anger at the world, anger at God; there are countless occasions for anger to rear its ugly head. It's an emotion that we all feel, and tend to feel the most often towards those we care about the most. The key is not to act out in anger, but to discover the root of your anger, and work through the grief that is left when your anger subsides. When you are overwhelmed, never let anger be in the driver's seat, it will only lead you deeper into chaos.

Refrain from anger and give up your rage; do not be agitated—it can only bring harm.

   Psalm 37:8

———

A patient person shows great understanding, but a quick-tempered one promotes foolishness.

   Proverbs 14:29

———

A gentle answer turns away anger, but a harsh word stirs up wrath.

   Proverbs 15:1

"But I tell you, everyone who is angry with his brother or sister will be subject to judgment. Whoever insults his brother or sister, will be subject to the court. Whoever says, 'You fool!' will be subject to hellfire."

Matthew 5:22

————

Be angry and do not sin. Don't let the sun go down on your anger, and don't give the devil an opportunity.

Ephesians 4:26–27

Lord, right now I am holding onto anger in my heart. Wipe this anger out of me. Give me the peace and patience that I need to forgive. Remind me daily of the forgiveness that You have given me. I'm afraid that if I let go of my anger I will not have anything left. I desire to love well, but I know I cannot do this without Your guiding hand. Grant me the wisdom to know how to handle this situation in love, and to know that letting go of my anger will not leave me empty, but give room for You to fill. Amen

ANXIETY

Anxiety can come up in every part of our lives. Beneath our anxieties is a need to feel in control. Control is impossible, and trying to hold on to it will only leave you scrambling and stressed. Our peace is found in knowing that the Creator of the universe holds us safely in the palm of His hand and will protect us no matter the situation in which we land. Release control to God, and allow yourself to be free in His hand.

"Therefore I tell you: Don't worry about your life, what you will eat or what you will drink; or about your body, what you will wear. Isn't life more than food and the body more than clothing? Consider the birds of the sky: They don't sow or reap or gather into barns, yet your heavenly Father feeds them. Aren't you worth more than they? Can any of you add one moment to his life-span by worrying?"

Matthew 6:25–27

———

Don't worry about anything, but in everything, through prayer and petition with thanksgiving, present your requests to God. And the peace of God, which surpasses all understanding, will guard your hearts and minds in Christ Jesus.

Philippians 4:6–7

"Peace I leave with you. My peace I give to you. I do not give to you as the world gives. Don't let your heart be troubled or fearful."
　　John 14:27

———

For God has not given us a spirit of fear, but one of power, love, and sound judgment.
　　2 Timothy 1:7

———

Humble yourselves, therefore, under the mighty hand of God, so that he may exalt you at the proper time, casting all your cares on him, because he cares about you.
　　1 Peter 5:6–7

Heavenly Father, no matter how much I wish it was not true, there are things that are outside of my control. I worry that I am not doing enough, or too much, or am not fully known or fully loved. I feel lost without some kind of control. Help me to leave my anxieties at Your feet. I entrust to You my anxieties, knowing that Your peace will guard my heart and mind. Amen

All of creation is ablaze with the beauty of the Lord. But sometimes it is easier to see than others. When you are constantly running through your to-do list, it is hard to take the time to see beauty. It is hard to imagine that anything will ever look beautiful again. And that is exactly when you need to see the beauty of God the most. Be intentional—look for it in sunsets, the night stars, and blooms of flowers. Find beauty in the midst of your chaos, and remember that God is with you.

*I have asked one thing from the L*ORD*; it is what I desire: to dwell in the house of the L*ORD *all the days of my life, gazing on the beauty of the L*ORD *and seeking him in his temple.*

Psalm 27:4

———

I will praise you because I have been remarkably and wondrously made. Your works are wondrous, and I know this very well.

Psalm 139:14

———

*Charm is deceptive and beauty is fleeting, but a woman who fears the L*ORD *will be praised.*

Proverbs 31:30

You are absolutely beautiful, my darling; there is no imperfection in you.
  Song of Solomon 4:7

———

Don't let your beauty consist of outward things like elaborate hairstyles and wearing gold jewelry, but rather what is inside the heart—the imperishable quality of a gentle and quiet spirit, which is of great worth in God's sight.
  1 Peter 3:3–4

Heavenly Father, I thank You and praise You for the beauty You have poured out on this earth, which heals and blesses the hearts that behold it. I am lost and need Your beauty to pull me back. Show me Your wondrous creation, and help me to never lose sight of the beauty that surrounds me, even in the darkest places. Amen

In the midst of stress it feels impossible to remember the blessings that God has placed in our lives. But even in the darkness, He is there. We can experience deep joy when we take notice of the abundant blessings in our lives and praise and thank the Lord for such bountiful grace, even in the midst of feeling overwhelmed. While running around, remember the provisions that God has given You.

"May the LORD bless you and protect you; may the LORD make his face shine on you and be gracious to you; may the LORD look with favor on you and give you peace."'

Numbers 6:24–26

———

Indeed, we have all received grace upon grace from his fullness, for the law was given through Moses; grace and truth came through Jesus Christ.

John 1:16–17

———

And God is able to make every grace overflow to you, so that in every way, always having everything you need, you may excel in every good work.

2 Corinthians 9:8

Blessed is the God and Father of our Lord Jesus Christ, who has blessed us with every spiritual blessing in the heavens in Christ.

Ephesians 1:3

———

And my God will supply all your needs according to his riches in glory in Christ Jesus.

Philippians 4:19

Heavenly Father, I thank You and praise You for all the ways You have shown me mercy and grace, and I ask for the blessing of Your presence throughout this day. I know that I could not get through this time of stress without Your outpouring of grace. Give me reminders today of Your goodness. Amen

Change is frightening. Whether you are mourning the loss of a loved one, preparing to leave a home you love, searching for a job, or even just finding yourself in a new stage of life, change can bring about high levels of stress. No matter what that change is, the presence of God goes before you preparing the way. Have confidence that on the other side of this change, no matter what the new world looks like, God will be there.

There is an occasion for everything, and a time for
every activity under heaven
    Ecclesiastes 3:1

———

"Do not remember the past events, pay no attention
to things of old. Look, I am about to do something
new; even now it is coming. Do you not see it?
Indeed, I will make a way in the wilderness, rivers
in the desert."
    Isaiah 43:18–19

"Because I, the LORD, have not changed, you descendants of Jacob have not been destroyed."
    Malachi 3:6

————

Therefore, if anyone is in Christ, he is a new creation; the old has passed away, and see, the new has come!
    2 Corinthians 5:17

————

Jesus Christ is the same yesterday, today, and forever.
    Hebrews 13:8

Lord Jesus, I do not know what the future holds for me, and it fills me with fear. I know that this stress is not the end of my story, and that You have a far greater plan ahead of me, but right now it is impossible for me to see. No matter what the future brings, may I take heart that You are with me until the end of the age. Bring me peace in the midst of this change, that I may not fear what is to come. Amen

None of us are immune from hardships, loss, and grief; but we can take heart that no matter what has happened, the Lord promises to comfort us. Sometimes He comforts us directly, sometimes through circumstances, and sometimes through the people He places in our lives. Think about the ways that God has comforted you in your times of need.

Even when I go through the darkest valley, I fear no danger, for you are with me; your rod and your staff—they comfort me.

Psalm 23:4

———

Remember your word to your servant; you have given me hope through it. This is my comfort in my affliction: Your promise has given me life.

Psalm 119:49–50

———

As a mother comforts her son, so I will comfort you, and you will be comforted in Jerusalem.

Isaiah 66:13

Blessed are those who mourn, for they will be comforted.

> *Matthew 5:4*

———

Blessed be the God and Father of our Lord Jesus Christ, the Father of mercies and the God of all comfort. He comforts us in all our affliction, so that we may be able to comfort those who are in any kind of affliction, through the comfort we ourselves receive from God.

> *2 Corinthians 1:3–4*

Dear God, thank You for comforting me and healing my heart in times of trial. I am lost in my grief and I know that the only way out is with Your comforting hand. Thank You for putting people in my life who bring me comfort. Guide me to those whom You have chosen for me as kindred spirits. Guide my actions that I may be a source of comfort for others. Use my life as a blessing for others. Amen

The Lord commands us to love our neighbors as ourselves and to also love our enemies—godly compassion is speaking and acting out of love in the best interests of others. Just like you would be willing to drop everything to help your dearest friend, you should be just as willing to have compassion for a stranger. This level of compassion is not possible on your own and is only possible through the Holy Spirit inside of you.

Yet he was compassionate; he atoned for their iniquity and did not destroy them. He often turned his anger aside and did not unleash all his wrath.

Psalm 78:38

———

When he went ashore, he saw a large crowd and had compassion on them, because they were like sheep without a shepherd. Then he began to teach them many things.

Mark 6:34

*Carry one another's burdens; in this way you will
fulfill the law of Christ.*

    Galatians 6:2

---

*And be kind and compassionate to one another,
forgiving one another, just as God also forgave you
in Christ.*

    Ephesians 4:32

Lord, may Your Holy Spirit fill my heart and soul with concern for my family, friends, neighbors, colleagues, and even enemies. Father, sometimes it is difficult for me to have compassion on those I consider deserving of their grief. Remove this hate from within me. Help me to see people the way You see them, and not through my own weaknesses. Open up my heart to the people around me that I may be a willing conduit of Your love. Amen

When we are under overwhelming stress, it can begin to eat away at our confidence. We allow ourselves to believe the lie that our worth is based upon what we can get done, and how in control we are. Remember that, no matter what challenges you may face, the power that created the universe and raised Christ from the dead lives inside of you. You have a greater power living inside of you than just your own ability to multi-task. You have the Holy Spirit.

Do not fear, for I am with you; do not be afraid, for I am your God. I will strengthen you; I will help you; I will hold on to you with my righteous right hand.
    Isaiah 41:10

———

It is not that we are competent in ourselves to claim anything as coming from ourselves, but our adequacy is from God.
    2 Corinthians 3:5

———

I am able to do all things through him who strengthens me.
    Philippians 4:13

So don't throw away your confidence, which has a great reward. For you need endurance, so that after you have done God's will, you may receive what was promised.

    Hebrews 10:35–36

———

This is how we will know that we belong to the truth and will reassure our hearts before him whenever our hearts condemn us; for God is greater than our hearts, and he knows all things. Dear friends, if our hearts don't condemn us, we have confidence before God and receive whatever we ask from him because we keep his commands and do what is pleasing in his sight.

    1 John 3:19–22

Heavenly Father, my stress is getting the better of me again, and I need Your help. I feel afraid and hesitant, but I know that with Your power I have no reason to feel this way. Grant me the kind of inner strength and confidence that only comes from trusting in Your love and provision for all my needs. Amen

At home, at work, in friendships, in families, in life—contentment is hard! We are constantly looking around to see what could be better, what we are missing out on, or what we used to have. The quickest route to contentment is through gratitude and trust: gratitude to God for what He has provided you and trust that He will continue to give you everything you need. Recognize the goodness in your life. See the good, and trust that God never fails to provide for your needs.

*"So don't worry, saying, 'What will we eat?' or
'What will we drink?' or 'What will we wear?'
For the Gentiles eagerly seek all these things,
and your heavenly Father knows that you need
them. But seek first the kingdom of God and his
righteousness, and all these things will be provided
for you. Therefore don't worry about tomorrow,
because tomorrow will worry about itself. Each day
has enough trouble of its own."*

   Matthew 6:31–34

———

*But godliness with contentment is great gain. For
we brought nothing into the world, and we can take
nothing out. If we have food and clothing, we will
be content with these.*

   1 Timothy 6:6–8

He then told them, "Watch out and be on guard against all greed, because one's life is not in the abundance of his possessions."

Luke 12:15

———

I don't say this out of need, for I have learned to be content in whatever circumstances I find myself. I know both how to make do with little, and I know how to make do with a lot. In any and all circumstances I have learned the secret of being content—whether well fed or hungry, whether in abundance or in need.

Philippians 4:11–12

Heavenly Father, thank You for Your unfailing love and faithfulness. Father, when I am lost in discontentment, push me to see all that You have provided for me. Do not allow me to continue to be blind, but open my eyes to the goodness that surrounds me exactly where I am. Grow in me a godly contentment, never wishing I was anywhere but exactly where You have placed me. Amen

DELIGHT

God is the only one who can bring you complete fulfillment and delight. While you are feeling the all-consuming weight of stress, look for the areas in life where God is still pushing you to smile. Delight in His Word, His creation, and in His presence.

How happy is the one who does not walk in the advice of the wicked or stand in the pathway with sinners or sit in the company of mockers! Instead, his delight is in the Lord's instruction, and he meditates on it day and night. He is like a tree planted beside flowing streams that bears its fruit in its season and whose leaf does not wither. Whatever he does prospers.

Psalm 1:1–3

———

He brought me out to a spacious place; he rescued me because he delighted in me.

Psalm 18:19

Take delight in the LORD*, and he will give you your heart's desires.*

Psalm 37:4

———

If your instruction had not been my delight, I would have died in my affliction. I will never forget your precepts, for you have given me life through them.

Psalm 119:92–93

———

"The LORD *your God is among you, a warrior who saves. He will rejoice over you with gladness. He will be quiet in his love. He will delight in you with singing."*

Zephaniah 3:17

Father, I am lost in the stress of life. I have become so focused on the needs of the future that I have lost sight of everything You have placed around me to bring me delight. Lord, open my eyes, remind me to smile; put Your Word on my heart, that I may delight in You alone. Amen

When your heart is heavy and your mind is burdened, hold fast to the truth that God comforts us in all of our afflictions so that we may be able to comfort others with His love. On our darkest days, Christ is there to lift us up into the light. When you find yourself lost in depression, allow these verses to fill your heart and bring you back to the truth.

The LORD sits enthroned over the flood; the LORD sits enthroned, King forever. The LORD gives his people strength; the LORD blesses his people with peace.

    Psalm 29:10–11

———

The LORD is near the brokenhearted; he saves those crushed in spirit.

    Psalm 34:18

———

Do not fear, for I am with you; do not be afraid, for I am your God. I will strengthen you; I will help you; I will hold on to you with my righteous right hand.

    Isaiah 41:10

*Answer me quickly, L*ORD*; my spirit fails. Don't hide your face from me, or I will be like those going down to the Pit. Let me experience your faithful love in the morning, for I trust in you. Reveal to me the way I should go because I appeal to you.*

Psalm 143:7–8

———

*I will give you the treasures of darkness and riches from secret places, so that you may know that I am the L*ORD*. I am the God of Israel, who calls you by your name.*

Isaiah 45:3

Dear Jesus, You were a man of sorrows and acquainted with stress—please fill my heart with Your strength and peace. Meet me where I am, and help me to find the way back into the light. My spirit is crushed, but I know You have saved me and will continue to do so. Be my strength when I am weak, my joy when I have none, and my light when I wander in darkness. Amen

DISCIPLINE

An essential path of growth is cultivating self-discipline: do the right thing at the right time in the right way. It is also the biggest way to alleviate stress. When you have a disciplined life, you do not need to worry about what will happen because you are already prepared in the places you have control and can leave the rest up to God.

Whoever loves discipline loves knowledge, but one who hates correction is stupid.

    Proverbs 12:1

The one who will not use the rod hates his son, but the one who loves him disciplines him diligently.

    Proverbs 13:24

Foolishness is bound to the heart of a youth; a rod of discipline will separate it from him.

    Proverbs 22:15

Instead, I discipline my body and bring it under strict control, so that after preaching to others, I myself will not be disqualified.

1 Corinthians 9:27

———

No discipline seems enjoyable at the time, but painful. Later on, however, it yields the peaceful fruit of righteousness to those who have been trained by it.

Hebrews 12:11

Heavenly Father, may Your hand guide me and correct me so that all I do and say will glorify You. Help me to live a life that is disciplined and steady. Give me the skills I need so that in the future I will not become stressed about the unknown. Amen

Feeling stressed can lead us into a feeling of dissatisfaction—either with our jobs, our families, or our lives overall. When you feel dissatisfied, it is often not because what you have is not enough, but because you have forgotten that only God can fully satisfy your soul. Rediscover the abundance around you by practicing gratitude and thanksgiving, even in the midst of chaos.

For he has satisfied the thirsty and filled the
hungry with good things.
 Psalm 107:9

———

You open your hand and satisfy the desire of every
living thing.
 Psalm 145:16

———

The LORD will always lead you, satisfy you in a
parched land, and strengthen your bones.
You will be like a watered garden and like a spring
whose water never runs dry.
 Isaiah 58:11

"I am the bread of life," Jesus told them. "No one who comes to me will ever be hungry, and no one who believes in me will ever be thirsty again."

    John 6:35

Now may the God of hope fill you with all joy and peace as you believe so that you may overflow with hope by the power of the Holy Spirit.

    Romans 15:13

Dear God, no good thing do You withhold from Your people. Help me see the goodness all around me and to delight in Your good and perfect gifts. Amen

God places people in our lives for a reason, and for our good. Seek out those who bring you encouragement. Pray for those you can bring encouragement to. Never hold in kindness that can be spread to lift up those around you. Even when you are stressed beyond measure, look for opportunities in life to cheer others up. You never know when those words are God pouring out encouragement through you to others.

The LORD is the one who will go before you. He will be with you; he will not leave you or abandon you. Do not be afraid or discouraged.

Deuteronomy 31:8

———

God is our refuge and strength, a helper who is always found in times of trouble.

Psalm 46:1

———

Aren't five sparrows sold for two pennies? Yet not one of them is forgotten in God's sight. Indeed, the hairs of your head are all counted. Don't be afraid; you are worth more than many sparrows.

Luke 12:6–7

I have told you these things so that in me you may have peace. You will have suffering in this world. Be courageous! I have conquered the world.

   John 16:33

———

And let us watch out for one another to provoke love and good works, not neglecting to gather together, as some are in the habit of doing, but encouraging each other, and all the more as you see the day approaching.

   Hebrews 10:24–25

Christ Jesus, may Your Spirit strengthen and encourage my heart today. Comfort me in my grief, and lift me out of my discouraged state. Show me those around me who need my encouragement. Place on my heart those friends who need a kind word today. Allow me to be the tool You use to help lift up everyone I meet today. Amen

Failure is part of life. It is not the failure in itself, but our ability to turn around, and use that failure. Unfortunately, it is too common for us to let our failures run our lives, to create unneeded stress remembering what happened last time. Though failures of any kind can crush our spirits, we have the assurance that God's purposes can never be thwarted. Walk in victory, knowing that any past failures are in the past, and God will use all to His glory.

*Now we have this treasure in clay jars, so that
this extraordinary power may be from God and
not from us. We are afflicted in every way but not
crushed; we are perplexed but not in despair; we are
persecuted but not abandoned; we are struck down
but not destroyed.*

    2 Corinthians 4:7–9

———

*He brought me up from a desolate pit, out of the
muddy clay, and set my feet on a rock, making my
steps secure. He put a new song in my mouth, a
hymn of praise to our God. Many will see and fear,
and they will trust in the LORD.*

    Psalm 40:2–3

And not only that, but we also rejoice in our afflictions, because we know that affliction produces endurance, endurance produces proven character, and proven character produces hope.

Romans 5:3–4

———

A person's steps are established by the Lord, *and he takes pleasure in his way. Though he falls, he will not be overwhelmed, because the* Lord *supports him with his hand.*

Psalm 37:23–24

Heavenly Father, grant me grace in times of failure and help me press forward as I fix my eyes on Jesus. Clear the failures from my mind, and do not allow them to cause me stress when I find myself in a similar situation. Thank You for the abundance of forgiveness You have poured over me. Amen

Fear comes in many forms; fear of the unknown, of the impossible, of broken trust. Any of these fears can be all consuming. But we have an almighty God who loves us and cares for us at all times. We have a powerful God who is strong through all things. We have an omnipresent God who never leaves us alone, and a God who is greater than any of our fears. With God on our side, there is nothing to fear, and nothing to stand in our way.

Haven't I commanded you: be strong and courageous? Do not be afraid or discouraged, for the LORD *your God is with you wherever you go.*
   Joshua 1:9

———

When I am afraid, I will trust in you.
   Psalm 56:3

———

You did not receive a spirit of slavery to fall back into fear. Instead, you received the Spirit of adoption, by whom we cry out, "Abba, Father!"
   Romans 8:15

For God has not given us a spirit of fear, but one of power, love, and sound judgment.

    2 Timothy 1:7

———

Humble yourselves, therefore, under the mighty hand of God, so that he may exalt you at the proper time, casting all your cares on him, because he cares about you.

    1 Peter 5:6–7

Abba, Father, I cry out to You for Your protection and comfort. I'm overwhelmed with fear. Fear of the future, and the unknown. I know that my fear stems from distrust, and that if I truly trusted You the way I say I do, then I would not have any fear. Thank You for Your faithful love and comfort. Continue to shelter me when I feel afraid. Amen

Forgiving someone who has hurt you means you no longer call to mind their fault or error—this extends grace to them and freedom for you. But it is not something that comes naturally, or easily, especially when the hurt has been caused by someone you trusted. This level of forgiveness is only possible by leaning on the Holy Spirit within you, and allowing Him to take control of cleaning your heart.

Therefore I tell you, her many sins have been forgiven; that's why she loved much. But the one who is forgiven little, loves little.

   Luke 7:47

———

Live in harmony with one another. Do not be proud; instead, associate with the humble. Do not be wise in your own estimation. Do not repay anyone evil for evil. Give careful thought to do what is honorable in everyone's eyes. If possible, as far as it depends on you, live at peace with everyone.

   Romans 12:16–18

*Be kind and compassionate to one another,
forgiving one another, just as God also forgave you
in Christ.*

    Ephesians 4:32

---

*As God's chosen ones, holy and dearly loved, put on
compassion, kindness, humility, gentleness, and
patience, bearing with one another and forgiving
one another if anyone has a grievance against
another. Just as the Lord has forgiven you, so you
are also to forgive.*

    Colossians 3:12–13

Dear God, it is easy for me to say that I forgive someone, but to actually release the resentment from my heart and let it be as if nothing ever happened . . . well I do not have any idea how to do that. Sometimes I feel trapped by the grudges and feelings of hurt that I have chosen to hold on to. I know that the feelings are not only damaging me, but my relationships as well. Please, just as You forgave all my debts and wrongs through Christ, empower me to extend forgiveness to those who have mistreated or hurt me. Amen

Friendship is not usually something that just knocks on your front door and stays forever. It needs to be invited, fostered, cared for, and encouraged. Precious are the friends, neighbors, and colleagues in our lives who faithfully stand by us through joys and sorrows, victories and failures, gains and loss. Find a way today to show the people in your life how much their friendship means to you.

Iron sharpens iron, and one person sharpens another.

> *Proverbs 27:17*

———

Two are better than one because they have a good reward for their efforts. For if either falls, his companion can lift him up; but pity the one who falls without another to lift him up.

> *Ecclesiastes 4:9–10*

———

Dear friends, let us love one another, because love is from God, and everyone who loves has been born of God and knows God.

> *1 John 4:7*

*No one has greater love than this: to lay down his
life for his friends. You are my friends if you do
what I command you. I do not call you servants
anymore, because a servant doesn't know what his
master is doing. I have called you friends, because
I have made known to you everything I have heard
from my Father.*

  John 15:13–15

———

*Therefore encourage one another and build each
other up as you are already doing.*

  1 Thessalonians 5:11

Lord Jesus, who called His disciples friends, thank You for demonstrating God's love for us and how best to love one another. Help me to be intentional in my relationships and to grow lifelong friendships. I thank You so much for the friends that You have placed in my life, and I pray that You allow me to be a blessing to them as well. Amen

When you are in a stressful situation, all of your emotions become heightened. It can become difficult to control your reactions. But remember that God has called us to a higher standard of self-control. By practicing gentleness, we can graciously approach people with a demeanor that reins in strength or assertiveness, regardless of the pressure we are feeling.

He protects his flock like a shepherd; he gathers the lambs in his arms and carries them in the fold of his garment. He gently leads those that are nursing.
　　Isaiah 40:11

———

Let your graciousness be known to everyone. The Lord is near.
　　Philippians 4:5

*The Lord's servant must not quarrel, but must
be gentle to everyone, able to teach, and patient,
instructing his opponents with gentleness.*
    2 Timothy 2:24–25

———

*Who among you is wise and understanding? By
his good conduct he should show that his works are
done in the gentleness that comes from wisdom.*
    James 3:13

Lord Jesus, You are the Good Shepherd who demonstrates gentleness to Your people. I am not capable of this gentleness on my own. Especially when my emotions get the better of me in stressful situations, I do not know how to show gentleness to those around me. May Your Spirit guide me in Your loving ways, and allow Your gentleness to flow through me. Amen

Grace is not deserved. It is not needed by the person who has always been reliable, or the child who has never been in trouble. The one who needs your grace is the friend who has cancelled on you four times this week, and now needs your help; the spouse who went on a shopping spree and forgot your birthday; the neighbor who complains about your lawn to others, and now needs help raking. How can you possibly bestow grace on these people? By the grace you have received from the Creator of the universe, you have the power to pass that grace on to others. The greatest gift we will ever receive is grace—the wholly unmerited favor of the Most High. Allow that grace to flow out of you to those who deserve it the least.

The law came along to multiply the trespass. But where sin multiplied, grace multiplied even more.
    Romans 5:20

———

For sin will not rule over you, because you are not under the law but under grace.
    Romans 6:14

———

Now if by grace, then it is not by works; otherwise grace ceases to be grace.
    Romans 11:6

But he said to me, "My grace is sufficient for you, for my power is perfected in weakness." Therefore, I will most gladly boast all the more about my weaknesses, so that Christ's power may reside in me.

    2 Corinthians 12:9

———

For you are saved by grace through faith, and this is not from yourselves; it is God's gift—not from works, so that no one can boast.

    Ephesians 2:8–9

Lord God, thank You for Your riches of grace that have been poured out on me through faith in Christ Jesus. I am left speechless when I think about all the repeated sin in my life that You have wiped clean. I know I do not deserve any of it, and yet Your grace abounds. Help me to show that level of grace to the people in my life. I know that only with Your strength will I be able to repay those who have sinned against me with grace. Amen

What does happiness look like to you? Is it a good book on the back porch? Or a hike in the mountains with your family? Maybe it's sitting around a campfire laughing with old friends. Though happiness sometimes comes from external circumstances, we experience the most lasting happiness by enjoying our union with Christ.

Therefore my heart is glad and my whole being rejoices; my body also rests securely.

Psalm 16:9

———

Take delight in the LORD, and he will give you your heart's desires.

Psalm 37:4

———

A joyful heart makes a face cheerful, but a sad heart produces a broken spirit.

Proverbs 15:13

I know that there is nothing better for them than to rejoice and enjoy the good life.

    Ecclesiastes 3:12

————

Rejoice in the Lord always. I will say it again: Rejoice!

    Philippians 4:4

Lord Jesus, I know that Your desire is for me to be happy. Align the desires of my heart with Your desires, so that I may find full and complete happiness. May my heart be happy and cheerful because I know You. Amen

It's tempting to put our hope in the wrong places—relationships, financial security, personal or professional abilities—but all of these will let us down and leave us broken. Our firmest hope is found only in Christ Jesus. He is our rock and firm foundation. When we are at the bottom, we know that ultimately He will save us from our brokenness and bring us back into the light.

Now may the God of hope fill you with all joy and peace as you believe so that you may overflow with hope by the power of the Holy Spirit.

    Romans 15:13

———

But those who trust in the LORD will renew their strength; they will soar on wings like eagles; they will run and not become weary, they will walk and not faint.

    Isaiah 40:31

———

I wait for the LORD; I wait and put my hope in his word.

    Psalm 130:5

We have also obtained access through him by faith into this grace in which we stand, and we rejoice in the hope of the glory of God. And not only that, but we also rejoice in our afflictions, because we know that affliction produces endurance, endurance produces proven character, and proven character produces hope.

  Romans 5:2–4

———

Let us run with endurance the race that lies before us, keeping our eyes on Jesus, the source and perfecter of our faith. For the joy that lay before him, he endured the cross, despising the shame, and sat down at the right hand of the throne of God. For consider him who endured such hostility from sinners against himself, so that you won't grow weary and give up.

  Hebrews 12:1b–3

Lord of hope, please fill me with all joy and peace as I hope in You. Hope is difficult when I am stuck in the midst of grief, and I know that it is only You that can give me the hope I need to find Your overflowing joy. Father, where grief dwells, Your hope abounds. Let my cup be so filled with hope, that no matter what hits me, only hope will pour out. Amen

Happiness can be fleeting, but joy is steadfast because it comes from the firm foundation of our intimacy with Christ. Because of this foundation, we have joy even in the darkest places. Build a strong foundation, so that when you are in your highest levels of stress, joy continues to pour out of your heart.

You reveal the path of life to me; in your presence is abundant joy; at your right hand are eternal pleasures.

Psalm 16:11

———

But the fruit of the Spirit is love, joy, peace, patience, kindness, goodness, faithfulness, gentleness, and self-control. The law is not against such things.

Galatians 5:22–23

This is the day the LORD has made; let us rejoice
and be glad in it.
    Psalm 118:24

———

As the Father has loved me, I have also loved you.
Remain in my love. If you keep my commands
you will remain in my love, just as I have kept my
Father's commands and remain in his love. I have
told you these things so that my joy may be in you
and your joy may be complete.
    John 15:9–11

Dear Jesus, thank You for the abundant joy that comes from Your faithful presence. I know that it's not possible for me to have this joy in my life without You. Please continue to pour joy into my heart so that it overflows into everything that I do. Amen

In God's great kindness, He saved us through His beloved Son, and He now calls us to extend that same gentleness and compassion to others, regardless of what excuses we come up with from our own lives. Look for opportunities, even in the midst of high levels of stress, to bestow kindness to those around you.

He also raised us up with him and seated us with him in the heavens in Christ Jesus, so that in the coming ages he might display the immeasurable riches of his grace through his kindness to us in Christ Jesus.

    Ephesians 2:6–7

———

Let all bitterness, anger and wrath, shouting and slander be removed from you, along with all malice. And be kind and compassionate to one another, forgiving one another, just as God also forgave you in Christ.

    Ephesians 4:31–32

Therefore, as God's chosen ones, holy and dearly loved, put on compassion, kindness, humility, gentleness, and patience.

    Colossians 3:12

———

But when the kindness of God our Savior and his love for mankind appeared, he saved us—not by works of righteousness that we had done, but according to his mercy—through the washing of regeneration and renewal by the Holy Spirit.

    Titus 3:4–6

Dear God, may Your Holy Spirit soften my speech and actions so that I display Your kindness towards everyone. I know I have failed and allowed my circumstances to take control of my reactions, but I want to repent and give my reactions over to Your control. Open my eyes to the opportunities around me to show kindness. Amen

A true leader isn't one who has climbed to the top of a hierarchy, but one who chooses above all else to be a servant to all. This leads to its own kind of stress, but as long as the leader you are following is Christ, you can leave all of your anxieties with him.

Jesus called them over and said, "You know that the rulers of the Gentiles lord it over them, and those in high positions act as tyrants over them. It must not be like that among you. On the contrary, whoever wants to become great among you must be your servant, and whoever wants to be first among you must be your slave; just as the Son of Man did not come to be served, but to serve, and to give his life as a ransom for many."

Matthew 20:25–28

———

Don't let anyone despise your youth, but set an example for the believers in speech, in conduct, in love, in faith, and in purity.

1 Timothy 4:12

Adopt the same attitude as that of Christ Jesus, who, existing in the form of God, did not consider equality with God as something to be exploited. Instead he emptied himself by assuming the form of a servant, taking on the likeness of humanity. And when he had come as a man, he humbled himself by becoming obedient to the point of death—even to death on a cross. For this reason God highly exalted him and gave him the name that is above every name, so that at the name of Jesus every knee will bow—in heaven and on earth and under the earth—and every tongue will confess that Jesus Christ is Lord, to the glory of God the Father.

    Philippians 2:5–11

Lord Jesus, You came not to be served but to serve—please grant me Your Spirit of servant leadership in all of my endeavors. Give me the confidence to know that everything I do is for You, and through You. Amen

PEACE

If you are at peace in all of your relationships, it is only a matter of time before conflict will arise. Rather than worry over what has happened in the past or what might happen in the future, be still with the Lord in the peace of the present moment. Be the one to ask for forgiveness, rather than holding on to resentment. Make the first step towards peace.

You will keep the mind that is dependent on you in perfect peace, for it is trusting in you.

Isaiah 26:3

———

For I am persuaded that neither death nor life, nor angels nor rulers, nor things present nor things to come, nor powers, nor height nor depth, nor any other created thing will be able to separate us from the love of God that is in Christ Jesus our Lord.

Romans 8:38–39

Peace I leave with you. My peace I give to you. I do not give to you as the world gives. Don't let your heart be troubled or fearful.

    John 14:27

———

And the peace of God, which surpasses all understanding, will guard your hearts and minds in Christ Jesus.

    Finally brothers and sisters, whatever is true, whatever is honorable, whatever is just, whatever is pure, whatever is lovely, whatever is commendable—if there is any moral excellence and if there is anything praiseworthy—dwell on these things.

    Philippians 4:7–8

Lord Jesus, I feel chaos and conflict in so many areas of my life. It is easy for me to be caught in the mess and forget the perfect peace that You have laid out for me. May Your perfect peace guard my heart and mind as I trust in You. Grant me the humility to seek out peace and be the one to lay down my pride at the feet of conflict, that my relationships may be redeemed. Amen

In the same way that our friendships and relationships with people need communication to be strengthened, so does our relationship with God. He has blessed us with the ability to speak to Him at all times, whenever we need Him. Especially when we are lost in grief, the best gift is dedicated time with our Creator. No matter how we come to the Lord, whether to present our requests or to sit silently in His presence, we can trust that He hears us.

"Whenever you pray, you must not be like the hypocrites, because they love to pray standing in the synagogues and on the street corners to be seen by people. . . . But when you pray, go into your private room, shut your door, and pray to your Father who is in secret. And your Father who sees in secret will reward you. When you pray, don't babble like the Gentiles, since they imagine they'll be heard for their many words. . . .

"Therefore, you should pray like this: Our Father in heaven, your name be honored as holy. Your kingdom come. Your will be done on earth as it is in heaven. Give us today our daily bread. And forgive us our debts, as we also have forgiven our debtors. And do not bring us into temptation, but deliver us from the evil one.

"For if you forgive others their offenses, your heavenly Father will forgive you as well. But if you don't forgive others, your Father will not forgive your offenses."

Matthew 6:5–15

If you remain in me and my words remain in you,
ask whatever you want and it will be done for you.
    John 15:7

———

Don't worry about anything, but in everything,
through prayer and petition with thanksgiving,
present your requests to God.
    Philippians 4:6

———

Pray constantly.
    1 Thessalonians 5:17

Lord Jesus, just as You taught Your followers how to pray, instill in me a deep desire to seek Your presence. Send reminders into my life of my need to spend time with You. Help me to remember to not only speak in my prayers, but to sit and listen to what You have to say to me. Give me rest in Your presence, that my spirit may be healed. Amen

Pride comes in many shapes and sizes. Arrogance tells us we are better than others, low self-esteem tells us we are worse, and praise makes us feel important; but they are all signs of pride, because they all put the focus on ourselves. Though we may be blessed with wisdom, success, and happy relationships, we can avoid pride by remembering that all good things are ours by the grace of God.

When arrogance comes, disgrace follows, but with humility comes wisdom.
Proverbs 11:2

———

Everyone with a proud heart is detestable to the Lord*; be assured, he will not go unpunished.*
Proverbs 16:5

———

A person's pride will humble him, but a humble spirit will gain honor.
Proverbs 29:23

Live in harmony with one another. Do not be proud; instead, associate with the humble. Do not be wise in your own estimation.

    Romans 12:16

———

For if anyone considers himself to be something when he is nothing, he deceives himself.

    Galatians 6:3

Father God, please forgive the ways I puff myself up rather than humble myself under Your loving hand. Help me to forget about myself, and keep my eyes on You. When I fall into a trap of pride, pull me to repentance, that I may not continue to sin against You. I know that any good I am capable of is only because of You. Amen

Chronic stress is quickly becoming a national crisis that threatens our health—but God is our ever-present helper in times of trouble. Lay your burdens at His feet, and do not allow yourself to become overwhelmed with the temporary problems of this world. Cast your burdens on Him, and He will carry you through this time of stress.

Cast your burden on the LORD, and he will sustain you; he will never allow the righteous to be shaken.
   Psalm 55:22

———

Commit your activities to the LORD, and your plans will be established.
   Proverbs 16:3

———

For I am the LORD your God, who holds your right hand, who says to you, "Do not fear, I will help you."
   Isaiah 41:13

Come to me, all of you who are weary and burdened, and I will give you rest. Take up my yoke and learn from me, because I am lowly and humble in heart, and you will find rest for your souls. For my yoke is easy and my burden is light.

Matthew 11:28–30

———

I am able to do all things through him who strengthens me.

Philippians 4:13

Dear God, please fill me and strengthen me with Your Spirit when I feel overwhelmed, exhausted, and uncertain. Give me peace during the stress. Remind me daily of what You have trusted me to handle, and what I need to lay down at Your feet. Help me to trust You and to know that nothing I do can ever get in the way of Your plan. Amen

TRUST

Trust is not an easy thing to give away.
Everyone has had a time when their trust has
been given to a friend, only to be betrayed. But
God is not a fallible human. To trust the Lord
is to believe what He has said about Himself:
He is good, faithful, and sovereign. He is
always worthy and deserving of our trust.

The person who trusts in the LORD*, whose confidence indeed is the* LORD*, is blessed. He will be like a tree planted by water: it sends its roots out toward a stream, it doesn't fear when heat comes, and its foliage remains green. It will not worry in a year of drought or cease producing fruit.*

    Jeremiah 17:7–8

———

I will be with you when you pass through the waters, and when you pass through the rivers, they will not overwhelm you. You will not be scorched when you walk through the fire, and the flame will not burn you.

    Isaiah 43:2

Wait for the LORD; be strong, and let your heart be courageous. Wait for the LORD.

    Psalm 27:14

———

And my God will supply all your needs according to his riches in glory in Christ Jesus.

    Philippians 4:19

———

This is the confidence we have before him: If we ask anything according to his will, he hears us.

    1 John 5:14

Dear God, thank You for working all things together for the good of those who love You and are called according to Your purpose. Thank You for being worthy of my trust and forgiving me when I question You. I praise Your matchless faithfulness. Help my disbelief. Amen

Our ability to work is a gift from God—we can create, serve, and produce for the good of the world around us, which glorifies the Creator. Everything that we do, we work at for the Lord, and not for ourselves. Because we are working with Him for His purpose, we can be confident that we will always succeed in His plans.

*Commit your activities to the L*ORD*, and your plans will be established.*
Proverbs 16:3

———

Do everything in love.
1 Corinthians 16:14

———

And God is able to make every grace overflow to you, so that in every way, always having everything you need, you may excel in every good work.
2 Corinthians 9:8

Whatever you do, do it from the heart, as something done for the Lord and not for people, knowing that you will receive the reward of an inheritance from the Lord. You serve the Lord Christ.

Colossians 3:23–24

———

Come now, you who say, "Today or tomorrow we will travel to such and such a city and spend a year there and do business and make a profit." Yet you do not know what tomorrow will bring—what your life will be! For you are like vapor that appears for a little while, then vanishes. Instead, you should say, "If the Lord wills, we will live and do this or that."

James 4:13–15

Creator of all good things, grant me meaningful work and empower me to do everything for You and not for people. Everything that I do, I work on for You. Lord, help me to give myself grace, and to not become overwhelmed with the stress of the tasks You have given me. Amen

Worry is false and useless fear—it's imagining and anticipating what might happen but probably won't. What can you change by worrying about it? Nothing. What can you fix by thinking about everything that could go wrong? Nothing. Instead, spend your time focused on today. On what you can do, on what you know to be truth, and leave the rest to God.

"*Therefore I tell you: Don't worry about your life, what you will eat or what you will drink; or about your body, what you will wear. Isn't life more than food and the body more than clothing? Consider the birds of the sky: They don't sow or reap or gather into barns, yet your heavenly Father feeds them. Aren't you worth more than they? Can any of you add one moment to his life-span by worrying?*"

Matthew 6:25–27

———

The Lord answered her, "Martha, Martha, you are worried and upset about many things, but one thing is necessary. Mary has made the right choice, and it will not be taken away from her."

Luke 10:41–42

We know that all things work together for the good of those who love God, who are called according to his purpose.

Romans 8:28

———

Don't worry about anything, but in everything, through prayer and petition with thanksgiving, present your requests to God. And the peace of God, which surpasses all understanding, will guard your hearts and minds in Christ Jesus.

Philippians 4:6–7

*Lord Jesus, I am often worried about many
things. I worry about tomorrow, about my family,
about what friends are really thinking, about
health, about clothes, about money, and about
countless other meaningless things. Jesus, I know
that my worry will do nothing, but the thoughts
are rooted in my mind, and I know I cannot
remove them without Your help. Remind me of
Your provision. Show me ways to let go of my
worry. Please grant me a heart like Mary, who
rested at Your feet. Amen*